First published in Great Britain in 2018 by Wayland

Copyright © Hodder and Stoughton Limited, 2018

Produced for Wayland by
White-Thomson Publishing Ltd
www.wtpub.co.uk

Series Editor: Georgia Amson-Bradshaw
Series Designer: Rocket Design (East Anglia) Ltd

ISBN: 978 1 5263 0650 0
10 9 8 7 6 5 4 3 2 1

Wayland
An imprint of
Hachette Children's Group
Part of Hodder & Stoughton
Carmelite House
50 Victoria Embankment
London EC4Y 0DZ

An Hachette UK Company
www.hachette.co.uk
www.hachettechildrens.co.uk

Printed in China

Picture acknowledgements:
Images from Shutterstock.com: Martin Vrlik 6tr, Dean Drobot 6br, NotionPic 7c, Second Banana Images 7br, boommaval 8, kostolom3000 9t, Michael C. Gray 9c, MriMan 9br, elenabsl 10tr, Irina Bg 11tr, phil Holmes 11bl, Sudowoodo 15c, Sapann Design 15b, Artram16b, arborelza 17, Sergey Yechikov 17bl, eveleen 18b, VectorPlotnikoff 19b, photoJS 23br, arborelza 24, Eric Isselee 25l. All illustrations on pages 12, 13, 20, 21, 26, 27 by Steve Evans

All design elements from Shutterstock.

Glossary words are shown in bold.

BOOM SCIENCE

HUMAN BODY

Georgia Amson-Bradshaw

WAYLAND
www.waylandbooks.co.uk

CONTENTS

HEALTHY BODY

Human beings have bodies that need to be kept healthy.

AMAZING ANIMALS

Human beings are a type of animal. It sounds funny, but animal is a scientific word for a living thing that can move around and breathe.

Hello, fellow animal!

BEASTLY BODIES

Like all animals, humans have a body. Our bodies are made up of different parts, such as our **bones**, our **muscles** and our **organs**.

STAYING ALIVE

All animals have the same basic needs in order to stay alive: food, water, air and warmth.

KEEPING HEALTHY

In order to keep our bodies properly healthy, we also need to do exercise, keep clean and eat a **balanced diet**.

HIDE AND SEEK

Getting enough sleep is also important to stay healthy. Can you spot a pillow hiding somewhere?

HEY, WHAT AM I?

This body part needs cleaning twice a day. What is it? Answer on page 28.

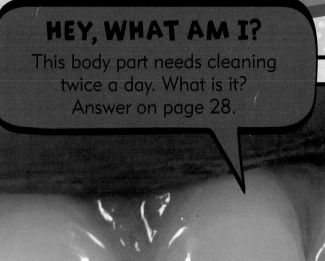

SKELETON AND BONES

Our skeletons hold our bodies up.

The **skull** is the name for the bones which protect the **brain** inside the head.

The **ribcage** is the set of bones that protects most of the organs.

The **spine** is the set of bones that run down the middle of your back.

THE BODY'S FRAME

Your **skeleton** is made up of all your bones. It holds your body upright and stops you collapsing into a wobbly pile on the floor!

WOW!

There are 206 bones in an adult's body. Nearly a quarter of those bones are in the feet and ankles, with 26 bones in each foot!

INSIDE ARMOUR

Your bones are very hard. Bones, such as your skull, act like armour beneath your skin. They protect your soft organs, such as your brain, from being damaged.

JOINTS

The places where your bones meet are called **joints**. Many joints, such as the ankle, elbow or hip, can bend or swivel. Our joints let us move around.

knee

hip

elbow

ankle

HEY, WHAT AM I?

An x-ray is a special type of photograph that lets you see your bones. Which part of the skeleton can you see in this x-ray?
Answer on page 28.

MUSCLES

Our muscles make our bodies move.

MUSCLE MACHINE

If your bones are like your body's hard frame, your muscles are a little bit like stretchy ropes. They are attached to your skeleton, and they move it around and hold it all together.

WORK IT!

When you use your muscles a lot, they get bigger and stronger. To keep your muscles healthy, it's important to get plenty of exercise.

HEY, WHAT AM I?

A few muscles aren't hidden underneath your skin ... What can you see in this picture? Answer on page 28.

PULL AND RELAX

Muscles can only pull, not push, so to move you around, they work in pairs. To bend your arm, the biceps muscle on top pulls tight, getting shorter and wider. The triceps muscle underneath relaxes and gets longer. To straighten your arm, the triceps muscle does the pulling.

WOW!

We use about 100 different muscles to speak.

Yes, I'm using 100 muscles, right now!

biceps muscle

triceps muscle

bone

See how the arm muscles work on the next page!

YOUR TURN!

MAKE A MODEL ARM

See how bones and muscles work together with this simple model of an arm.
You'll need:

Two 30 cm rulers

Sellotape

Selection of rubber bands, including two large ones

STEP ONE

Overlap the two rulers at the end, so that about 3 cm of each sticks out beyond the point they are overlapped. Hold them in place by criss-crossing some small elastic bands around the area that is overlapped.

STEP TWO

Loop the two large elastic bands around the top end of the upright ruler, and tape them in place. Stretch one elastic band so it loops around the longer side of the crossways ruler. Stretch the other elastic band so it loops around the short side of the crossways ruler.

STEP THREE

Pull on each large elastic band in turn to see how it moves the model arm up and down. Can you see how one 'muscle' stretches as the other one is pulled shorter?

DIGESTIVE SYSTEM

We take goodness from our food during digestion.

EATING WELL

Food is fuel that gives our bodies energy to run, and the **nutrients** it needs to repair itself. We need to eat the right sorts of food to stay healthy.

As soon as she looks away, the food is mine!

A healthy diet includes lots of fruit and vegetables, some starchy foods such as bread or pasta, and some **protein** from eggs, nuts, beans, meat or cheese.

THE FOOD JOURNEY

The food we eat goes through our **digestive system.**

1 First, we chew the food into small pieces with our teeth.

2 We swallow the food down the **oesophagus**.

3 In our **stomach**, the food is mashed with **acid**. This breaks it down even more.

4 The **liver** helps break down fat in our food.

6 Finally, in the large intestines, water is absorbed and the rest becomes waste, called **faeces**.

5 In our small **intestines**, the nutrients are **absorbed** into our **blood**.

WOW!

The intestines are about 6.5 m long. That's as long as four grown-ups lying head to toe!

HEART AND BLOOD

Blood carries useful things around the body, and collects waste.

WOO! I'm feeling PUMPED!

FLOWING AROUND

Blood is a sticky red liquid that flows around our bodies. This flowing movement is called circulation. It is driven by a big muscly pump: the **heart**.

OXYGEN

DELIVERY SYSTEM

Blood is like the body's delivery system. As it flows around the body, it carries useful things such as oxygen to the places it is needed. It also carries waste away so the body can get rid of it.

VEINS AND ARTERIES

The heart is connected to a network of thin tubes that the blood flows through.

The tubes that carry blood away from the heart are called **arteries**.

Veins carry blood back to the heart, to be pumped around again.

the heart

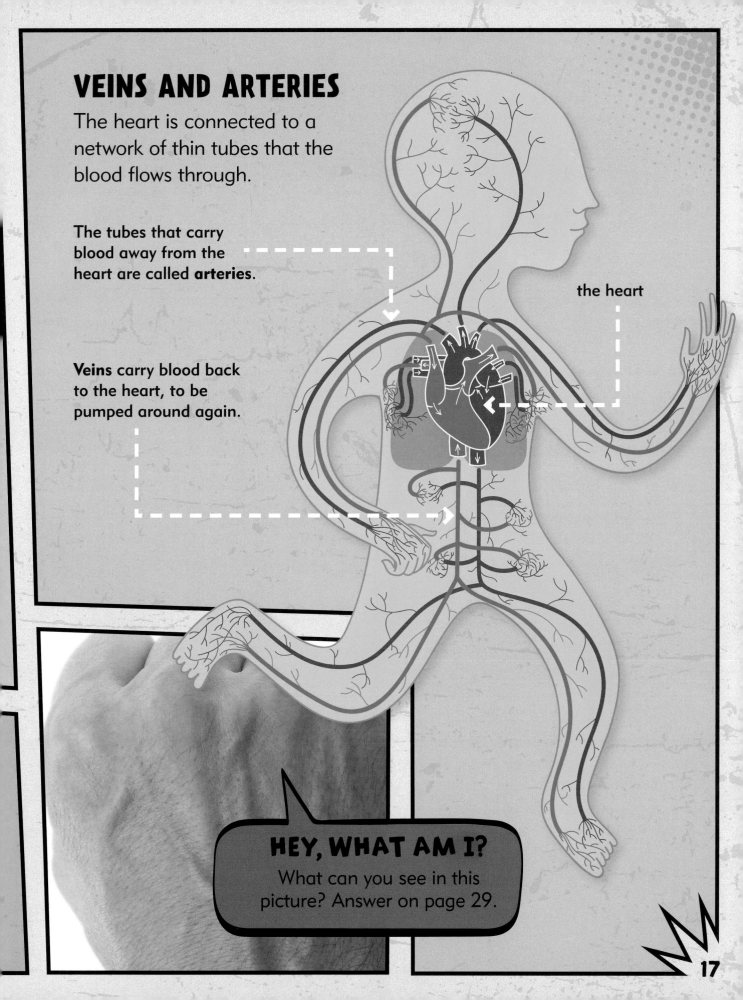

HEY, WHAT AM I?
What can you see in this picture? Answer on page 29.

BREATHING

We take in oxygen through our lungs when we breathe.

You take my breath away!

LUNGS

The **lungs** are a pair of pink, spongy organs full of tiny air sacs. Beneath the lungs is a dome-shaped muscle called the **diaphragm**.

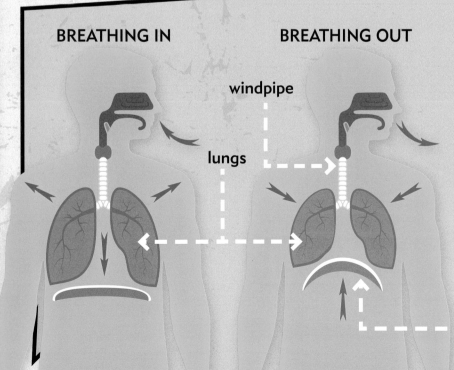

BREATHING IN

BREATHING OUT

windpipe

lungs

diaphragm

HOW WE BREATHE

When we breathe in, the diaphragm moves downwards and flattens out, making our lungs draw in air and get bigger. When we breathe out, the diaphragm relaxes upwards again.

GAS IN

Air contains a gas called oxygen that we need to stay alive. When we breathe air into our lungs, the oxygen passes from the air into our blood.

GAS OUT

Our bodies also produce a waste gas called carbon dioxide. When we breathe out, we get rid of this waste gas into the air around us.

WOW!

A grown-up's lungs can hold about 6 litres of air. That's like three big fizzy drink bottles.

HIDE AND SEEK

We breathe in through our mouth. What else do we breathe through? Can you find it hiding?

YOUR TURN!

HOW BIG ARE YOUR LUNGS?

Test how much air your lungs can hold with this fun experiment. You'll need:

Some flexible plastic tubing

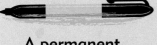

A permanent marker pen

A two-litre plastic bottle

Water

A measuring jug

A large plastic tub

STEP ONE

Using the measuring jug, fill up the two-litre bottle with water, 250 ml at a time. Each time you add another 250 ml, mark the water level on the side of the bottle with the marker pen.

Ask an adult to help you with this experiment

STEP TWO

Fill the tub about two-thirds full with water. Holding your hand over the top of the two-litre bottle so no water can escape, turn it upside down and put it into the tub of water. The open end should be under water, and the bottle still full of water.

STEP THREE

Holding the bottle steady, poke one end of the plastic tubing into the open end of the bottle under the water.

STEP FOUR

Take a deep breath, and then blow it all out down the tube. The air will push some of the water out of the bottle. Using the marks on the side, measure how much air (in ml) is now inside the bottle. This is how much air your lungs can hold!

SENSES

Our senses tell us what is going on around us.

EYES AND SIGHT

We see things with our eyes. This is our **sense** of sight. It tells us things such as the shape and colour of objects around us.

NOSE AND SMELL

When we breathe in through our nose, we can smell things. Our sense of smell tells us things such as if food has gone off.

22

EARS AND HEARING

We hear sounds with our ears. Our sense of hearing helps to tell us what is happening around us.

TONGUE AND TASTE

We taste our food with our tongue. Taste buds on our tongue sense different flavours.

SKIN AND TOUCH

Our skin covers our whole body. We can feel things against our skin. This is our sense of touch.

HIDE AND SEEK

Can you spot a pair of blue eyes hiding somewhere?

HEY, WHAT AM I?

This part of the body is linked to one of the senses. Can you name the body part and the sense? Answer on page 29.

BRAIN AND NERVES

The brain controls the rest of the body.

the brain

NERVE NETWORK

The brain is like the body's command centre. It is linked to the rest of the body by a network of **nerves**. These are pathways that carry information to and from the brain.

The spinal cord is a thick bundle of nerves connecting the brain to other parts of the body.

WOW!

It takes 1/1000th of a second for a signal to travel from your toe to your brain.

nerves in leg

MAKING SENSE

Our eyes, ears, mouth, nose and skin are connected to the brain by our nerves. They send signals to the brain, which takes the information and turns it into an overall picture of what is going on around us.

The eyes are reporting a brown thing. The ears are hearing a barking noise. I think it's a dog.

Right foot - STEP!
Left foot - STEP!

MAKING MOVES

As well as receiving information, the brain sends out instructions. Signals travel along our nerves to our muscles, telling them to move.

YOUR TURN!

TEST YOUR SENSES

Test your sense of sight, touch, taste and smell with these three activities. You'll need:

Two flavours of yoghurt

A selection of differently-shaped objects, such as a pine cone, ball, sponge, and so on

A blindfold

A friend

OOOOOOOOOOOOOOOOOOOOOOOOO
OOOOOOOOOOOOOOOOOOOOOOOOO
OOOOOOOOOOOOOOOOOOOOOOOOO
OOOOOOOOOOOOOOOOOOOOOOOOO
OOOOOOOOOOOOOOOOOOOOOOOOO
OOOOOOOOOOOOOOOOOOOOOOOOO
OOOOOOOOOOOOOOOOOOOOOOOOO
OOOOOOOOOOOOOOOOOOOOOOOOO
OOOOOOOOOOOOOOOOOOOOOOOOO
OOOOOOOOOOOOOOOOOOOOOOOOO
OOOOOOOOOOOOOOOOOOOOOOOOO
OOOOOOOOOOCOOOOOOOOOOOOOO
OOOOOOOOOOOOOOOOOOOOOOOOO
OOOOOOOOOOOOOOOOOOOOOOOOO
OOOOOOOOOOOOOOOOOOOOOOOOO
OOOOOOOOOOOOOOOOOOOOOOOOO
OOOOOOOOOOOOOOOOOOOOOOOOO
OOOOOOOOOOOOOOOOOOOOOOOOO
OOOOOOOOOOOOOOOOOOOOOOOOO

STEP ONE
SIGHT

How good are your eyes? Look at this block of letter O's. Hidden somewhere among them is a letter C. Can you find it?

STEP TWO

TASTE AND SMELL

How do your sense of taste and smell work together? Ask an adult to help you with this activity. Get your friend to put on a blindfold and ask them to hold their nose so they can't smell. Without telling them which is which, ask them to taste the two flavours of yoghurt. Can they guess the flavours correctly? Try again without them holding their nose.

STEP THREE

TOUCH

Is your sense of touch the same all over your body? Put on the blindfold. Ask your friend to gently press each of the different objects against your skin on different areas of your body such as your elbow, the palm of your hand, and so on. Can you correctly identify each object?

That tickles!

ANSWERS

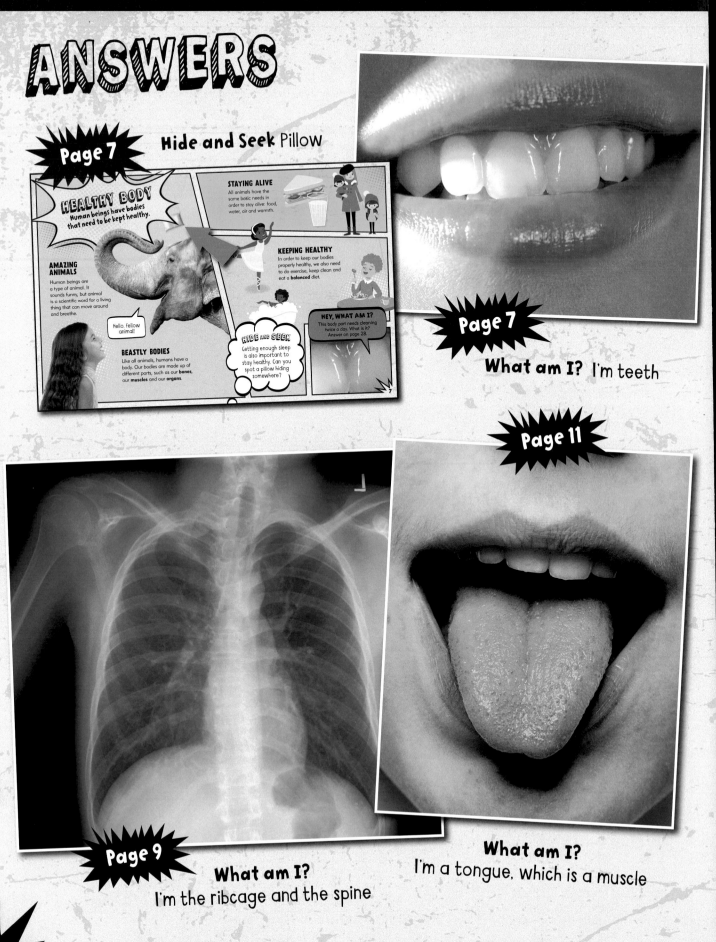

Page 7

Hide and Seek Pillow

Page 7

What am I? I'm teeth

Page 11

What am I?
I'm a tongue, which is a muscle

Page 9

What am I?
I'm the ribcage and the spine

Page 17

What am I?
I'm veins and arteries in the hand

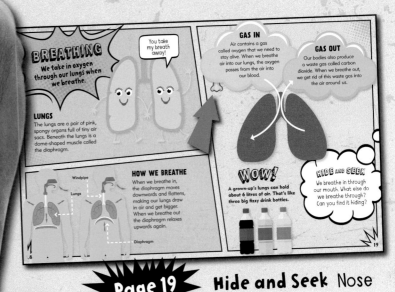

Page 19

Hide and Seek Nose

Page 23

What am I?
I'm an eye, used for sight

Page 23

Hide and Seek
A pair of blue eyes

Page 26

Sight test
The letter C is 12 lines down and 10 letters in from the left.

GLOSSARY

absorb to take in or soak up

acid a liquid in the stomach that helps break down food

arteries tubes in our bodies that carry blood away from the heart

balanced diet a diet that contains all the different nutrients we need to be healthy

blood a sticky liquid that carries nutrients and oxygen around our body to where they are needed

bones the different parts that make up our skeleton

brain a squishy organ inside the head that acts as the control centre for the body

diaphragm a muscle that sits underneath the lungs to help us breathe in and out

digestive system the organs that process our food

faeces the waste part of food that has been digested

heart a muscly organ that pumps blood around the body

intestines long tubes that make up part of our digestive system where nutrients and water are absorbed from our food

joints parts of our skeleton where two or more bones meet

liver an organ that helps break down fat in our food

lungs spongy organs inside the chest that we use for breathing

muscles the stretchy parts of our body that attach to our bones and let us move around

nerves very thin pathways that send information around the body

nutrients the goodness in food

oesophagus the tube in our throat that goes from the mouth to the stomach

organs parts of our body that have a particular job

protein a type of nutrient that we need in our diet

ribcage the bones that make a cage protecting many of our important organs, such as our heart and lungs

senses the abilities we have to take in information from the world around us

skeleton the hard frame that holds the body up

skull the hard bones of our head that protect the brain

spine the bones that run down our back and let us stand up straight

stomach a bag-like organ where food is mashed up so we can absorb its nutrients

veins thin tubes that carry blood towards the heart

INDEX